APPROXIMATELY PARADISE

APPROXIMATELY
PARADISE

floyd skloot

TUPELO PRESS

First paperback edition September 2005
Library of Congress Control Number 2005903085
Tupelo Press
PO Box 539, Dorset, Vermont 05251
802.366.8185 • Fax 802.362.1883
editor@tupelopress.org • web www.tupelopress.org

Cover art *Summer at Mission Lake* by Beverly Hallberg.

Cover and text designed by William Kuch, WK Graphic Design

✻

Tupelo Press is an award-winning independent literary press that publishes fine fiction, non-fiction and poetry in books that are as much a joy to hold as they are to read.

Tupelo Press is a registered 501(c)3 non-profit organization and relies on donations to carry out its mission of publishing extraordinary work that may be outside the realm of the large commercial publisher.

We are most grateful to Ronni J. Leopold for contributions to the press that made possible the publication of *Approximately Paradise*.

For Beverly

Open your eyes
To the good blackness not of your room alone
But of the sky you trust is over it,
Whose stars, though foundering in the time to come,
Bequeath us constantly a jetsam beauty.

—Richard Wilbur, "Walking to Sleep"

ACKNOWLEDGMENTS

Some of these poems first appeared, sometimes in different form, in the following publications:

Bellevue Literary Review: "Midnight in the Alzheimer's Suite"
Black Mountain Review (Ireland): "The Geology of Home"
Canary River Review: "The Newlyweds, 1938"
Center: A Journal of the Literary Arts: "Interrupted Melodies"
Cobweb (Ireland): "Snap-Apple Night"
Colorado Review: "The Travels of Esther Houston"
Crazyhorse: "Circles"
Cyphers (Ireland): "The Newlyweds, 1938"
Gulf Coast: "Scrapbook"
Hotel Amerika: "Still November"
The Hudson Review: "Dress Rehearsal" and "Recurrence"
Image: A Journal of the Arts and Religion: "Gauguin in Oregon"
The Iowa Review: "Heat Wave" and "Soft Flame"
Iron Horse Literary Review: "The Witness Tree"
Margie: "Carson McCullers at the Spinet," "The Keyboard Trial," and
            "Yeshiva in the Pale, January, 1892"
New England Review: "François Couperin's Secret Harpsichord"
New Letters: "Lunch in the Alzheimer's Suite"
Notre Dame Review: "Cezanne's Studio, 1901"
Poetry East: "The Last Ball" and "The Long Hall"
Prairie Schooner: "American Camp, San Juan Island"
Pivot: "Snap-Apple Night"
Quarterly West: "Quarter-Moon Over Achill Island"
Rhino: "The Geology of Home"
Salmagundi: "John Constable at Sixty, London, 1837"
The Sewanee Review: "Patrick Kavanagh at First Light" and
            "Thomas Hardy at Bockhampton"
Shenandoah: "Brahms in Delirium" and "Striking the Set"
The Southern Review: "James McNeill Whistler at St. Ives"
Southern Poetry Review: "Under an August Moon"
Tar River Review: "The Juncos' Dance"
Virginia Quarterly Review: "Relocation," "The Role of a Lifetime," and
            "Salmon River Estuary"
Washington Square: "Reese in Evening Shadow"

"Circles" and "The Last Ball" were reprinted in *JAMA: The Journal of the American Medical Association.*

CONTENTS

I LOST NOTES

*A darkness in the weather of the eye
is half its light*

–Dylan Thomas, "A Process in
the Weather of the Heart"

THE ROLE OF A LIFETIME

I am bound upon a wheel of fire
–King Lear

He could not imagine himself as Lear.
He could do age. He could rage on a heath.
Wounded pride, a man gone wild: he could be clear
on those, stalking the stage, ranting beneath
a moon tinged red. Let words rather than full
throated roars carry fury while the wind
howled. He could do that. And the awful pull
of the lost daughter, the old man more sinned
against than sinning. The whole wheel of fire
thing. But not play a wayward mind! Be cut
to the brains, strange to himself, his entire
soul wrenched free, then remember his lines but
act forgetting. Understand pure nonsense
well enough to make no sense when saying
it. Wits turned was one thing; wits in absence
performed with wit was something else. Playing
Lear would force him to inhabit his fear,
fathom the future he had almost reached
already. Why, just last week, running here
and there to find lost keys, a friend's name leached
from memory. Gone. No, nor could he bring
himself to speak the plain and awful line
that shows the man within the shattered king:
I fear I am not in my perfect mind.

RECURRENCE

He remembers walking across that hill
last year. It is lost now in a froth of mist
as he sits in bed minding the crude twist
of morning light through haze. Nothing will
change fast enough for him to feel it where
he needs to feel it most. He looks and there
is only more white whispering that time
has truly stopped. From the limb of an old
growth oak just beyond view he hears the cold
notes of a barred owl's hoots, a simple rhyme
he takes to mean the worst. The air is still,
heavy as the breath in his chest. He knows
this moment well enough by now to close
his eyes and picture sunlight on the hill.

GAUGUIN IN OREGON

In relapse again, I have been dreaming
of my body buried in white blossoms
that flutter from the bitter cherry,

soft as the spring breeze and scent
of hyacinth wafting through the screen,
accompanied by a sound like the strokes
of a brush on canvas.

                                 An owl?
Deer browsing the hillside trails?
No, the winter creek still surging.

I think I am awake now.

                             Between rains,
finespun mist drifts among the oak
and swaying fir, a ballet choreographed
in dreamtime, costumed in black
and gray. The music, I realize, is made
from shades of dawn, is all cloud,
delicate as the creamy crown
of an early daffodil.

                           My eyes close again,

but then I see him move.

                            Gauguin!
I would know him anywhere. My size,
my age, but looking fresh from a wrestle
with angels. I was reading about him
only yesterday.

Saffron-colored shirt
like a glimpse of sun, fringe of hair tangling
where I thought to see leaves, bandy legs
unsteady on the sloping land, he reaches
as if grasping one last fruit of the dark.
Where his stained hands slash through a web
of clouds, colors bleed together, stars vanish.

He radiates rage. I sit up against the headboard,
blinking, naked in a snarl of white sheets.
I know I am awake now.
                              His form tells me
Gauguin expects to find himself again
in an island paradise. The sort of place,
he wrote, where *Life is singing and loving.*
The afterlife as advertised to the child
he was in Peru, as dreamed by the seaman
he became in the frozen north, as sketched
by the heartsick wild-man dying on Dominique.
A century dead, he must be more sensitive
to cold than ever. Surely he knows by now
that paradise is approximate.
                                    Though he lusts
for heat and seething tropical morning light,
here those vapors dancing before his eyes
will have to do. He stalks his way east
toward the crest, lush with Turk's lily
and wild iris. Their sudden color stops him.

Gauguin, if I am not mistaken, is hearing
inner music, a vibration of blues and golds,
the pure vermilion resonance he remembers
as the color a cello turns when played

in its deepest register. I see the savage
glee in his eyes as he looks around,
forgetting where he is in time
to find the lone lilac about to bloom.

Thirst stirs in him. Hunger.
                              He died
at fifty-five, dreaming of food and wine,
and I am fifty-five, dreaming of burial
by fruit trees that bear no fruit.
Lost in time, back in bed since the dead
of winter, I have woken in the dark
in absolute certainty that it was seven
years ago. Then, in a heartbeat, five
years from now.
                    I must walk to Gauguin
before he vanishes. Against a hazing sky,
he is already growing light and I go out
where the morning colors gather.

CARSON McCULLERS AT THE SPINET

Against New York winter light, the hiss
of passing tires and rants of New Year's drunks,
her Chopin nocturnes always conjured
Georgia nights with Mama and Brother-Man.
Cream sherry tinted gold by candleflame.
Plates of steamed artichokes and clarified
butter in etched cups, their scents mingling
with a languid Chattahoochee River breeze,
toothpicks jutting from the cubed hearts.
Moody bird-chatter under the melody line.
Smoke in the air and the breath of family
everywhere. She could make the harsh
northern seasons flow without notice
over the stones of time, her music slow
and sultry while crisp darkness took hold.

Now, after three strokes, she is only cold.
She sits at the spinet, the stiffened claw
of her left hand folded deep in her lap.
Straight ghostly fingers flash across
cracked keys, still sharp in the upper
register, and she hears the familiar melodies,
but none of it is real. Her good eye
sees the shadowy silhouette of a Christmas
tree flicker in a draft near the window.
Frost flowers on the panes. When no one
else is there, she will unfurl her fist and dare
the simple left-hand of a Scarlatti sonata.
She will seek a Schubert song, her strong
soprano voice flooding the lost notes.

BRAHMS IN DELIRIUM
Vienna, 1890

He hears the sound of sunset as a cello
and snowflakes as flutes above a soft wind
of clarinets. All the reds and yellows
of a fall afternoon are oboes in his mind.

He knows he is out of his mind. He hears
the swift percussion of his racing heart
and feels it carry him toward what he fears
most, the end of all his music, the start

of everlasting silence. Faint harp notes
burst to the surface of each breath. He strips
to the waist, crosses the room. His face floats
in the washstand's mirror and water drips

down his flushed cheeks, his beard. He sees
an overturned jug hover above his head.
Now all it holds are a few melodies,
a passage in strings for all the unsaid

words, a theme shredded like winter light
as the snow ceases to fall. Then, nothing.
Silence will at last fill the room, and night
come on with its own secret songs to sing.

FRANÇOIS COUPERIN'S SECRET HARPSICHORD
Paris, 1732

In the room beyond the room
where Couperin composed suites
for roving shadows and butterflies,

in the time after music
stopped for good and his heart grew
thick with trapped rhythms,

in darkness lit only by a trio of tapers
Couperin conjured his perfect harpsichord.

Its case was shaped like the wings
of angels, but lean and flowing
as though honed for long flight.

Made of poplar brushed to the luster
of cypress, the body would glow
with all he remembered of dawns
spent composing at his sycamore desk,

of Paris streets in moonlight, or the vast
breath filling a young bagpiper's chest.

He would test each iron wire string,
match each slip of wood to its proper
quilled tip. Eyes closed, hands poised,
he imagined each plucked tone living
to linger on the air, resisting decay.

That should be the sound heard in heaven.

Some days his lungs seemed to fill
the room with their yearning and all
he could do was rest. He heard
above the frightened linnet of his wheezing
the sound light would make
if only it could find its way into music.

Those days, knowing himself to be
deep in the brief coda of his years,
Couperin saw himself painting
the thinnest gold leaf band on the lid,
testing the joints of the wrestplank
papering the smoothed interior
as a blossoming orchard where songbirds
thrived. One night he would paint a breeze.
One night the melody of the Seine.

He would give days to the bone and black
oak keyboard. Down on the floor
with parchment and veneer, he would shape
a rose for the hole in its flowered soundboard.

All would be balance. All would be clean
and dry. He never knew how much longer
to worry about the color of sound,
the poise of touch. But near the end,
as his fevers rose, he dreamed in counterpoint,
seeing four sets of hands move across
the upper manual, all his, all longer
and wiser than at any time in his life.

HEAT WAVE

Soaring on still wings, head naked and red,
a turkey vulture circles four donkeys
in a field gone to seed. It rides a gust
of August wind that rattles the plum trees'
coppery leaves and whirls a sudden dust
devil up through the hazy afternoon light.
Spooked, a foal stops grazing, canters away
from the herd and turns at the fence to bray.
One thin cloud drifts like the tail of a kite
from the sun now directly overhead.

STILL NOVEMBER

Nothing moves under the Hunter's Moon.
This light is a threat. There is something
still but grimly poised in the air
and its silence holds the season's worst news,
just a slight shift in wind, a pressure
change felt where your breathing begins.

But nothing like a storm, not even drizzle,
only November's held breath at the turn
toward winter. An inkling of clouds
massing below the horizon, which may be
nothing more than the folly of memory,
the sense that what happened each year
since you came here must happen again.

SOFT FLAME

He recognizes no one in his dreams.
The brother is not his brother, the child
not his child. His wife, all amber light, streams
through a window that is not there. A wild
current of wind warms the night and he sees
he is no longer himself either. June,
bitter cherry blossoms drift from the trees
to form clouds that slowly cover the moon,

and somewhere he can hear himself calling
in a voice that is not his voice. His name
fills the night, rising with light and falling
around him like the blanket of soft flame
that is his wife whispering him awake,
beckoning him to the brink of daybreak.

II THE HARD TRUTH

DRESS REHEARSAL

His second act costume weighs fifteen pounds,
and he must dance in it under hot lights
while singing with an alto whose voice sounds
like a full moon blazing on summer nights.

Smiling all the while, he must project ease,
the wit of a rogue prince whose true passion
is for battle, and grace enough to please
this young partner. But his face is ashen,

brow drenched. Breath is elusive as the birds
he tries to describe in this endless song.
He stops. If he could recall the rhymed words
that take him offstage now, he would be gone

for good. Nothing comes to him. There are wings
everywhere, action shattering the still
moment he hoped to create. Hazy rings
of light, behind which an audience will

be applauding at this time tomorrow,
fade as he awaits the falling curtain
now, lost in a soft, rapturous sorrow
where nothing moves and nothing is certain.

YESHIVA IN THE PALE, JANUARY, 1892

Early morning, as Cossacks on horseback
circled the old wooden synagogue, chants
seeped out like smoke through the walls. Black
hatted elders inside shut their eyes and danced
in circles of their own before the holy ark.
Prayer deepened the air as one fat soldier nailed
the Tsar's seal to the door: CLOSED. Then a spark
cast from somewhere near the rising sun sailed
across the wintry sky, encircling soldier
and temple, nuzzling rooftree, gable, beam.
It found the place where mingled rage and dream
were draft enough to let a wildfire smolder.
One moment shadows questioned the winter dark
and next moment the answer arrived in flame.

THOMAS HARDY AT BOCKHAMPTON

At birth the doctor gave him up for dead,
setting him on the hearthstone. But the nurse
saw breath. It was a sudden blaze of spirit, she said,
more light than air. She knew he was its source

and snatched him up as the room filled with cold
fire. She felt in her bones he would be old
before his time, saw him haunted by strange
shapes, darkness within the avid dance of flame.

She watched him grow as though penned in a cage.
His hopes tangled in shadow by the back
door, their loss tinged with the scent of lilac.
Then woodland and sullen heath became

his heart's home. Bent oak, furze, a rose's thorn
would always mean the place where he was born.

THE KEYBOARD TRIAL
Rome, 1709

Scarlatti as oft as he was admired for his great execution
would mention Handel, and cross himself in veneration.
                              –Rev. John Mainwaring, 1760

Scarlatti stalked the Cardinal's inner court.
He already had enough to worry
about, and now they were making a sport
of playing harpsichord. He must hurry
to the crowded private chambers and greet
Handel, the Saxon, as though they were not
close friends. He must smile and bow and compete
against a man who could play like a god.

The Cardinal called it a trial. Everyone
knew what a trial meant in the Roman Church.
Sooner call it a duel. *Let us have fun,*
the Cardinal said, and Scarlatti would search
those icy eyes while thinking that such gifts
as Handel's were possible at the hands
of heaven only. The way incense drifts
over a nave, or sunlight dries the sands

as the tide recedes, the way wind rises,
that is the way Scarlatti feels the hands
of heaven himself, and it surprises
him each time it happens. He understands
what it means to lose the Lord's touch. But men

like Cardinal Ottoboni, so lavish
in his faith, or Handel time and again
writing and playing music to ravish

the soul, were oblivious of the fear
that could haunt Scarlatti before a blank
score or gleaming keyboard. Only last year
he thought his fingers, swollen in the dank
air of his rooms, might never recapture
their former grace. Last week, emptied of all
melody, he wondered if the rapture
of song was a dream he might not recall.

He knew the time had come. From deep within
the walls he heard the Cardinal call his name
and knew in a moment he must begin
moving toward the room lit by candleflame.
He closed his eyes to become the long limbs
of a poplar whose lacquered wood became
the perfect harpsichord awaiting him
as the Cardinal again called out his name.

JAMES McNEILL WHISTLER AT ST. IVES
Cornwall, 1883

Whistler needs no one to sit for him now.
He is finished with portraits, with people.
Finished with nocturnes too, soft edges,
the muted light of a coastal fogscape.
He needs surprise. He wants to be outside
with a panel of wood, a thumb box of colors
and brushes, and nothing to hold him in place.
Bring on the war of sea and shore, clouds
blown apart. Autumn daylight like a shock
to the heart stirs him to life. He is after
the spontaneity of a breaker turned back
on itself. What is a whitecap but a stroke
of wind on wave, the Lord's own breath
in a flash of foam? Away too long from storm,
from the sea's surge, he feels himself awaken
before the horizon's shifting form, where time
itself is visible to the naked eye, where a ship
caught in a trough struggles to right itself.

JOHN CONSTABLE AT SIXTY
London, 1837

Alone in the city, alone with memories
of Maria and their home on the heath,
Constable closes his eyes to find the sky
very close to his heart now. If he could
paint what he has come to know of it,
he would leave out the high blues,
leave out the watery violet that daylight
makes of a late winter afternoon
and the sea's azure embrace on clear
summer days. There will be no more
of these for him. He would rely on reds
now, the heavenly blood that warns
of storms, the blush rushing west
to east from the depths of a hidden sun.
His heart's hue. He would turn to reds
for their tint of certain loss on a day
otherwise full of promise, the hard truth
he learned from his wife's glazing eyes.
He would turn away from the comfort
of graying cumulus, the flicker of shadow.
It is his pleasure to imagine himself at last
one with the sky. But he will paint nothing
again, feels nothing calling him out
of his swollen heart. In the city, he feels
so much older than his years, as though aging
two for every one Maria has been gone.
What he remembers is that it took so long
for him to look up from the landscape,
to forget those paired swans on the lake

at Wivenhoe Park, scattered cattle at pasture,
visible dew and breeze, wildflowers in bloom
along a fold of hill, the distant copse,
the mill, the sprawling manor house.
But once he saw the sky for what it was,
the sky was all he could see. It was the spirit's
true shade, the Lord's lyric cry a man alone
heard and never forgot. Till now. The sky
is gone from his sight, taken into his body,
and all that remains is in tatters above
the city's dark buildings as he walks,
lost in thought, always looking down.

HOME REPAIRS

The summer he wallpapered his daughter's
bedroom, rain finally buckled the back deck
and sluiced the loose roof shingles free to
flutter off on a gust of wind. He knew
what was happening before his eyes, how water
goes for what holds an old house together
and tears it apart from the outside in.
So does the sun. A week of record heat
seemed to draw the house in upon itself
as he steamed, peeled and scraped through sheet
after sheet of tulips, roses, toy soldiers
and prancing horses. He could hear the thin
cry joists make as they dry. He worked by himself,
a storm of plaster around his shoulders,
the air thick with mold and age, nothing left
to mark the past but bare wall, a tapestry
of cracks, and a door that would not stay closed.

THE LONG HALL

The old man only wants to walk
the hall. He cannot smile. He goes
from locked door to blazing windows
and back, fists clenched, able to talk

of nothing but his need to get
out. Blind in light, he scowls and turns
back. The dark at the far end turns
out to be a door again, yet

his faith in escape never dies.
As long as he moves there is hope.
Light and dark, a kaleidoscope
blanched and turning in his mind's eye—

the shut door, the windows ablaze,
the long hall with its sparkling walls,
closed rooms, and the shadow that calls
his name as he walks down the days.

UNDER AN AUGUST MOON

This is the Green Corn Moon. This is the end
of summer rising with heat in its fat red fist.
Stars shoot through the night. The trend is
toward lingering high pressure off the coast.
By day, flat blue skies; by night, stillness
growing darker, denser. Power fails.
Mars has come near and looms to the south.
There is something starker than ever
to this August, an eloquence in its fever pitch.
Speech fails to convince. We want thunder
and heavy rain but get lightning strikes
and wildfires. The peace is broken,
deserts of the east in flames, the west
torrid with terror. Promise turns threat
and the heavens press upon us.
This is the error of our ways.
The corn crop stands scorched in its ears.
The sun saying we have learned nothing
will stare us down in the morning.

III THE ALZHEIMER'S SUITE

Memory is a primary and fundamental faculty, without which none other can work; the cement, the bitumen, the matrix in which the other faculties are imbedded; or it is the thread on which the beads of man are strung, making the personal identity which is necessary to moral action.

–Ralph Waldo Emerson, *"Memory"*

LUNCH IN THE ALZHEIMER'S SUITE

My mother smiles at me. She reaches out
to touch my face and wonders who I am.
The fleck of tuna dangling from her mouth
falls as she asks "Can you find me a man?"
Swaying willow and afternoon drizzle
fracture the light that falls across her tray.
Her hands, as though assembling the puzzle
lunch has become, adjust fork, bowl and plate,
adrift in shadows. Sometimes she forgets
to swallow. Sometimes she holds a spoonful
of soup in the air and loses herself
in its spiraling steam. In a whirlpool
of confusion she may suddenly sink
in her seat and chew nothing but thin air.
She is fading away. Her eyes grow dark
as she looks at the old man sitting there
claiming to be her son. She slowly shakes
her head, lifts an empty cup and drinks.

MIDNIGHT IN THE ALZHEIMER'S SUITE

Lost in the midnight stillness, my mother
rises to dress and begin another
chilly day. She crosses the moonlit floor.
There is too much silence beyond the door,
and a lack of good cheer, so she breaks
into song. But the coiling lyric snakes
back on itself and tangles in her throat.
She stops long enough to see a cloud float
along the hall, but somehow the cloud speaks
in the voice of the night nurse. Someone peeks
from a doorway. Now someone starts to moan,
someone else coughs and my mother's stray song
returns for a moment: *oh you belong
to me!* If the audience would quiet
down, she would remember. Opening night,
that's what this must be, and the curtain parts,
and the spotlight is on, the music starts,
but there is too much movement, too much noise,
yet she cannot stop, must maintain her poise,
smile and keep on singing. Then it must be
over because the night nurse is there, she
embraces my mother and leads her back
offstage, whispering, bringing down the dark
again. Tired, but pleased with her last set,
my mother lies down for a well-earned rest.

RELOCATION

Thirty thousand feet above the Badlands
my mother looks out her window and says
"There's a car beside us." She understands
for a moment that we are flying, prays

aloud for the pilot to find his way
through all this dark. Then she asks why
the chairs in our hotel are so small today.
She says there is something in my eye

and brushes her finger across the lid
of her own. Seeing the papery skin
loose on the back of her hand, its grid
of wrinkles, she blinks and asks again

how old she is. When I say she is ninety,
she looks away, sees the engine, turns
back and grabs my arm. She asks if I see
the car, then whispers that she yearns

to go upstairs to her room and invites
me to join her. There is nothing I can do
to help her through the long nights
ahead, nights strange as this afternoon

when we cross the country together.
Though she can no longer live alone,
I realize that no matter where my mother
lives now, she will always be alone

in a world forever gone wild in her mind.
Still thinking I am her last late boyfriend,
she leans closer, says "you're always so kind
to me" and sighs as she pats my hand.

THE LAST BALL

My mother, drifting loose in time,
is waltzing at the Tsar's last ball.
Her costume sparkles with Fabergè
gems in the dying winter light.

She has come at ninety to the core
of her dreams, the dark place before
her life began, where she can twirl
in a prince's arms, Yiddish forgotten,

fluent in tongues that speak of love
alone. She is luminous with beauty,
ablaze as the music moves within
the plaques and tangles of her brain.

CIRCLES

My mother has lost her way
through time and memory,
turning circles down a dark
hall where past and present
diverge. Footsteps of the child
I was echo and fade. My brother,
dead one year, calls in a voice
she no longer recognizes. All
around her drift fragments
of song, lost melodies, a final
dazzling trill held beyond belief.

The world outside these walls
has ceased to matter, its petty
demands stacked on her desk
and sealed in their crisp white
silences like obedient children.
That desk now sits flush under
a nursing home window shut
for good against the sound
of the sea. Blinds are drawn
to block light winking off surf.

VIRGIN ISLANDS
Spring, 1963

My mother sits beside me in the plane,
hands clenched on the armrests as we descend
toward the Caribbean. *This is the end,*
she whispers. *The pilot must be insane.*

I watch the sea, blistered by whitecaps, fill
with our shadow. No white sand beaches
anywhere. No land. My mother reaches
her breaking point, shuts her eyes and shrieks *we'll*

all die! as the plane touches down. Not yet
sixteen, I am dressed in tropical white
as we step into burning island light,
and I try to hide the black circle etched

on my pants' pocket by the eager condom
in my wallet. The sun seems to have set
a ridge of low hills ablaze to the west,
and kindled the winds that come in random

loops from the shore. My mother wears the bright
clothes of her second year as a widow.
Back in her life, she looks in the window
of the terminal, glad to still be alive,

composing herself while I drift away.
A young woman and I look at each other
in passing before I meet my mother
at the taxi for our drive to the bay.

THE NEWLYWEDS, 1938

They began with a waltz in the Sky Gardens
of the Hotel St. Moritz. Her gown glittered
as she spun through light and he moved
like her shadow, a perfect fit but a fraction
behind the beat. Her eyes were closed.

His eyes were open wide, seeing black
circles afloat in haze above their heads.
It was only a trick of light and shadow
and the motion of a crystal chandelier.

For a week at sea they sampled the rumba
and haughty paso doble. Her sequined cape
as it swished was supposed to sparkle
but the ship's lamps lacked candlepower.
Between dances they circled the deck
and smoked in the open air. She bent
her face to his cupped flame, lifted her face
to the light of a waning moon, and watched
from the corner of her eye as he drifted
into and out of floating shadows of cloud.

Too soon they landed in Cuba but she tried
holding onto the music. In scarlet sundress
and flopping hat she sashayed down
the rickety dock. She twirled and glided
from warehouse shadows into narrow streets
ignited by the moon as he watched—
as she imagined everyone watching

from the Sans Souci windows and verandas
of the Casino de la Playa. They would catch
at once the rhythm of her silent samba.

He lingered too long behind her looking
away, soaking up the sudden aroma of fresh
cigars and rum. In the flare of a streetlight
she saw his steps in the square become
a prizefighter's dance of defense, hands hiding
his face, footwork deft enough to make her
heart flutter before darkness claimed him again.

SCRAPBOOK

In all her childhood photos that survive,
my mother wears a costume of some kind:
a scowling gypsy with her tambourine;
chauffeur in worn livery poised to drive
a cardboard roadster; bold pirate, half-blind,
before an ocean painted on a screen.
At Coney Island, with her young brother
wearing his suit, she is dressed as a Greek
goddess, I think, with gleaming crown, leather
leggings, and shield. Here beside her mother
on the beach, she lounges sheathed in a sleek
dress and flapper's hat with one long feather
dangling past her shoulder. She never smiles
and she never appears to be a child.

IV INTERRUPTED MELODIES

SALMON RIVER ESTUARY

Drifting close to shore, we enter the shadow
of Cascade Head. Our kayak jitters in an eddy
as we dip and lift the double-bladed paddles
to keep ourselves steady. Lit by morning sun,
current and rising tide collide before our eyes
in swirls of foam where the river becomes
the sea. Surf seethes across a crescent of sand.
Gone now the bald eagle's scream as it leaves
a treetop aerie, the kingfisher's woody rattle,
gulls' cackle, wind's hiss through mossy brush.
Light flashing through sea mist forges a shaft
of color that arcs a moment toward the horizon
and is gone. Without speaking, moving together,
we power ourselves out of the calmer dark
and stroke hard for the water's bright center
where the spring tide will carry us back upriver.

THE TRAVELS OF ESTHER HOUSTON

Late that summer Esther Houston set out
in her swaying red Olds to see the parks
before they lost their green. She had no doubts
about that youthful doctor and his stark
predictions, his scans and films with gaping
holes, the plastic skull with its yolk of brain
exposed to show there was no escaping
her fate. But she was not in any pain
yet, could still eat and sleep, and was ready
to hit the road.
        When the time came, when she
lost her way or her hands were not steady
enough, James could drive, or their daughter Leigh,
or a chauffeur. She loved the thought of that,
her James unable to believe his eyes
when a driver in uniform and hat
arrived. Then she thought: *like death in disguise,*
and shook her head to clear it of the dark
ideas that sometimes caught her half asleep.

She sat down and made a list, one state park
per week, one national park, places deep
in forest and teeming with hidden life.
Esther yearned for water, too, rushing streams,
river water cutting rock like a knife
and disappearing from sight in a beam
of foamy light.
        At seventy, she found
it hard to believe there was still so much

beauty she had missed, all that sacred ground
left to visit now, before she lost touch
altogether.
            She could reach the ocean
and be home in a day. James would want to
cover her ears against the commotion
of waves; this time she would tell him not to
and hoped he would understand. That would be
near the end anyway, the sea. Her first
trips would have to be east to see the trees.

James seemed bemused because he feared the worst
when Esther sat him down to talk about
her plans. Hoarded pills and plastic bags filled
his dreams; though she knew he was a devout
man, James lived in terror of what might build
up inside her, what she might ask him to do.

But driving twice a week to bring her peace
was easy work. Pay the fee, see the view,
take her home again.
                    James missed the soft fleece
of his wife's hair, her ample flesh, that grace
she had in movement, but her laugh remained,
and the struts of reason were still in place,
and he wanted to keep her entertained
as long as he could. He thought it would take
no more than a month till she had to stop.

They began with the park at Mission Lake
whose ranger was the last son of a cop
Esther knew from her years at City Hall.
They greeted each other by name when James

bought their one-day pass, and Esther was all
bubbly, like a child, describing the scenes
she hoped to see. The ranger waved them through.

That was the first sign James had. She was worse
already. Everything she saw was new
though she saw it all before. The world burst
upon her with each moment and she seemed
to love it, but forgot it in a flash.
He wondered if it returned when she dreamed
or was gone for good.
      The next week she asked
for Mission Lake and greeted the ranger
in his Welcome booth with cries of pleasure.
She said, you expect a total stranger
and find a friend. This world is all treasure,
James, if you just know how to look at it.
The trail beside the river, the great blue
heron nesting on the bank and soft chip
of a lazuli bunting were all new
once again. Shocked by her wild joy, grieving
even as he thanked the Lord for this small
touch of mercy, James knew she was leaving
him behind while he watched and it was all
he could do to keep up with her last brief
lessons in how to live.
      On the fourth week,
stopping to examine a fallen leaf
she found lying at the edge of their street,
Esther told him their travels were over
by turning around and floating upstairs
like a ghost. Settled under the covers,
she smiled at James and pointed to the chair
before her vanity. He moved it near

the bed and watched her close her hazel eyes
as though hoarding the sight of what was dear
to her. Call Leigh, she whispered.

                                               Her first sighs
convinced him of what he had not allowed
himself to know. She would not eat again,
or drink. She would not cry, or speak out loud.
She would not want anything more of them
than to let her go.

INTERRUPTED MELODIES

In the cramped living
room of a Bed
and Breakfast in British

Columbia, a parrot at
dawn whistles only
the first seven notes of the

theme from "Bridge On
the River Kwai" and lures
us to the edge

of sleep, waiting
without knowing we are
waiting for the next

note that never
comes to
complete the melody.

This is the way
to begin a summer
vacation as light

wavers just beyond
our window and we are
now fully awake

when the first
four notes from
"I Could Have Danced

All Night" are brought
short before those
fourth and fifth

notes we know are
there but have been
withheld as the parrot

chortles, pleased with
himself, having done his
duty, having left us

yearning.

QUARTER-MOON OVER ACHILL ISLAND

One June evening in 1926,
as a Jack Russell terrier
crossed this ridge of bog,
the moon suddenly wagged

its slender tail and burst
into tears. This brought
the dog to a halt as all
around him tufts of gorse

took flight toward the one
star aglow above Slievemore.
Then he reared back to bark
down the wind for he had seen

wind carry worse things away
before, but soon the foothills
filled with his mangy cousins
and he knew he had failed.

The night, gleaming with
manic light, broke free.
Eagles that gave this place
its name swooped through

a sky now dappled as the dogs,
and everywhere was the sharp
odor of burning peat despite
a long afternoon's heat.

No one in the dark village
could sleep again that night.
They tossed in their beds
except for one strange child,

eyes glazed by joy, who began
climbing a ladder of purest
longing toward the empty space
that was the source of his dreams.

SNAP-APPLE NIGHT
All Hallows Eve in Ireland, 1833

On Snap-Apple Night the barn's gloom is green
with smoky light. Chairs dangle from rafters
and sway above the skirt-swishing dancers.
The blacksmith sings as a fiddler careens
into the space where a woman just leaned
over to quench the piper's thirst with beer.
Haloed by the music and candlelight,
a child kneels at an oak bucket to snap
after the evening's last windfall apple.
Beyond him, near the fire, two lovers face
away from the song's question. They are still
as no one else is. Her downcast look will
never change, never soften toward the Yes
that fills the landlord's barn this cold fall night.

AMERICAN CAMP, SAN JUAN ISLAND

Word spreads that all three eaglets seem ready
to soar. We watch one flap at the nest's rim
and settle again. The mother's steady
gaze gives nothing away, but she wants him

to rise, that much is clear, and she is not
going anywhere until he does. June
mornings here should not be so still or hot,
the young deserving spring breeze and skies strewn

with high clouds for their first flight. Fledging done,
and the great basket of their nest growing
smaller by the day, and summer light come
early, and a crowd of tourists showing

up: soon there is another brawl of wings.
This time his talons clear the nest before
he drops again and his soft chitter rings
down like a feather to the forest floor.

SHAW ISLAND LANDING

In late June, swirling
wind remembers spring
storms still draping
the Olympic range.

Sunlight finally finds
us as the ferry turns south.
A broken clock on the port
wall says twelve past
midnight or noon.

Seawater foams
to port. Ahead of us,
an aging nun in dark
habit and red windbreaker
waits at the far end
of the dock to bless
all passengers
as they come and go.

THE WITNESS TREE

They sat on a ragged four-patch quilt,
lulled by light frisking the grapevines
and high grass. Contrails criss-crossed
the afternoon sky, which reminded
them for a moment of watching the war
on television. But soon someone insisted
they taste the ninety-eight winemaker's
reserve and someone else said the late
shadows bore an odor of chardonnay
across the hill's crest. They nibbled
smoked Edam in a gathering silence.

When dusk quickened they noticed
nothing. The landscape ruffled once
like a nervous cat and settled back
toward stillness. Purple and white lilacs
fluttering in a sudden whorl of wind
woke them enough to reckon the air,
sharp now with ozone, that drew taut
before a distant rumble like the echo
of clouds massing. Then lightning split
the witness tree right before their eyes.

CEZANNE'S STUDIO, 1901

Black clock without hands
on a cloth creased by folds.

The folds, deep as chasms,
more lustrous than the room's
bare light. Near the edge,

a water-stained crystal vase
with one scarlet rose petal
sprawled over its cracked lip,

a lemon draped in mold
and dusk lurking behind lace
curtains that hang like aging flesh

above the sink. This ominous
calm, shadow within shadows.

Backwards on its easel,
a sketch in ink: the cracked dome
of a skull, waxy and amber
as the candle nub beside it,

where we expect apples
in a bowl. Eye and nose holes
like spots of rot loom darker
than anything else there,

even empty space below
the table, even stains where fire
licked the candlestick,
even the clear, cold night.

STRIKING THE SET

After the last curtain falls
and the audience has gone
the characters drift back
onstage, dressed for the real
world again. They wander
the set, makeup caking necks,
an eye shadowed, a face
streaked with dark creases.

The young man who played
an aging bachelor still slouches
in character, his temples grayed
but a light now wild in his eyes.
The mail clerk/disgraced soldier
flashes a disposable camera
from the wings. The widow
and her tall killer husband
have hammers in their hands
and are smiling in a way
no one in the cast recognizes.

But everyone waits, some in tears,
others impatient to be gone.
A small chorus standing stage left
finally harmonizes on the lyric
blown tonight in Act Two.
From his seat in the back row,
the Director lifts his customary
closing night bottle of Bourbon,
freeing them to bring down
the world they made together.

V ROYAL SUMMER

HOMECOMING

The place he always hoped to live
waits just beyond this crest.
He knows he is close,
though a twist of cedar smoke
is all he can see of it.

Stopping to rest,
he lets a crust of soda bread
soften on his tongue
as he thinks
how all those wrong turnings
matter so much less
now that the end is in sight,

those nights alone
in cabins open to the skies,
that fraying rope
of muscle in his back,
the early pace
that could not have been held
by a man half his age,
a lack of water, a lack of light.

Up ahead the evergreen thin
and straggle, tips snagging
late afternoon mist.

The hour is lost
but at last he can see
where bare land begins
in a scatter of ancient till.

There among the cobbles
and boulders, in a flicker
of shadow over the saxifrage,

he knows nothing is left
but wind to contend with.

THE GEOLOGY OF HOME

We live on the limb of an overturned fold,
a shadow zone come late afternoon
when the crest is set ablaze. Just past
the hinge line wild blackberry thrives,
draping itself around a bed of stones.
Nothing is ever guaranteed here.
The compressed earth beneath our house
can heave and bend like a lamb at play,
young enough to change in a flash.
This morning, in a windless moment,
I saw stillness gather itself and abandon
first the grass, then the blotched iris,
tulips, fennel, twin oaks, feathery cirrus
and finally the faint crook of a quarter moon.

PATRICK KAVANAGH AT FIRST LIGHT

I am king/Of banks and stones and every blooming thing.
—Patrick Kavanagh, "Inniskeen Road: July Evening"

Through my bedroom window I see the old
man rise from his knees as though floating
on shadows. He comes and goes as I waken,
clear for a moment among the oak and pine,
then gone, then back where the bank folds
in a tangle of blackberry vines on the hillside.

His large hands sift a palmful of soil as he stares
into the distance and hears, I imagine, the call
of the dawn train headed south. This late
in July, morning climbs the horizon in fits
and starts. I turn over. From five miles away,
a car's headlights sweep the valley and flash
Kavanagh's hunched shadow against my wall.

Then I am beside him. The brim of a battered
fedora hides his eyes. As he brushes his hands
together, scattered dirt catches in the cuff
of his pants. He dislodges a rock from its niche
between us using the worn edge of his boot heel
and mutters *I see your land is only tumbled stones
and a worrying wind.* "Like Inniskeen," I tell him.
"So you should feel right at home here."

At that my wife stirs and sighs. So I have gone
nowhere after all, and realize I have been talking
to myself. Except there is Kavanagh again, quick
as a finch, perched atop an Adirondack chair

near the yarrow just coming into bloom.
He glares at daybreak's bittersweet glow
now seeping through the leaves and spreads
his arms. *A mile of kingdom,* he whispers
into the sudden breeze. I know there is nothing
he would not give for one more royal summer
in the country of light. Drifting back to sleep,
I hear him move east through a break in the trees.

AMITY HILLS

I came here uneasy with the strange ways of forest life,
the crying sound of a white oak swaying in winter wind,
            mellow huff of deer settling to sleep
                   on a slope, the soft rain—
         after sunset has spread like a stain—
becoming sudden storm rushing through the valley as night
falls, or the steady return of wildness across a thin
                margin we have made to keep
         ourselves still within the seasons' wax and wane.

And I was slow to fathom the loudmouth tree frogs' bright green
exuberance in underbrush as the pond rose with March
            runoff. Never knew what fog looked like
                   from above, or how it seeped
         through leaves like the spirit of a breeze.
What dawnlight does to the dew trapped on a torn windowscreen.
I had not slept outdoors or lost myself under an arch
                of fir and climbed the hillside's
         contours home. I never felt as free

as the evening grosbeak bursting like flame from a snowdrift
in late November, as the maple trapped in its cycle
            of reddening but soon enough to
                   begin budding. Life was slow
         to change here but change would go
on endlessly, and seldom seemed to change pace. Morning mist
sometimes formed itself into a blazing rainbowed circle
                above our house and would do
         a kind of dance before it was through

with us. I never knew how connected weather was to
the tint of leaf, or light was to where coyote crossed a hill,
        time was to the space a forest claimed
                for deadfall. Till, near fifty,
      I finally left the city
and went to be with my love in her round house in the woods,
where soil was hard, water deep, and the late June air was cool.
             We live where nothing is tame,
      above a small town called Amity

at the stony end of an ancient lava flow, on massed
rock left by Ice Age floods. Poison oak and blackberry vines
        thrive here. By year's end a creek will rise
              from the hill's heart and pour
      for six months upon the valley floor,
dwindling back underground when the summer solstice has passed.
Time here has drawn me out beyond strangeness. Or drawn me in.
          I have learned that surprise
      is not always shock and nothing to fear,

that the dark-eyed juncos throng when wild fennel goes to seed,
that Indian summer can color the landscape of dreams
        gold through a winter of freeze and thaw,
            that the pattern of wind
      and the way old growth trees have been thinned
together help a harsh September rain carve itself deep
into the ridge exactly where evening sun always seems
          to soften the least flaw
      in all we see before the dark begins.

THE JUNCOS' DANCE

Trilling in the early April light,
a flock of dark-eyed juncos flits
from swaying feeder to lilac
to sword fern to cedar sapling
and back. A solitary jay watches
from his barberry perch, bobbing
as though in time to their reel.
I have seen him commandeer
the feeder, scattering sunflower
seeds and millet in moody squalls,
twitching his crest in triumph,
one grain caught in his beak.
I have heard his call, this brash
punk, a voice half hawk, half crow.
But now, his blue-gray feathers lit
by morning sun, he simply sits,
mesmerized before the common
elegance of the juncos' dance.

RALLY IN JUNE
Amity, Oregon

At Third and Trade a Model A
waits to turn left. It's a hiboy
two-door from the Hoover years, gray
as the hair and old corduroy
cap its driver sports. He wears thick
goggles that sparkle in the sun.
A Nash the color of glazed brick
pulls up behind and toots its horn,
joined by a four-door Hupmobile
and Dodge touring car with a man
who looks asleep behind the wheel.
They wait for a Packard sedan
which is waiting for us to cross
the street. Here we are, all frozen
in time, the noon heat like a gloss
laid over what we have chosen
to do with a summer Sunday,
watching a past none of us knew
gather together in the shade
of a small village park in June.

REESE IN EVENING SHADOW

I prayed for easy grounders
when Pee Wee Reese fielded,
hanging curves when he hit.
At Ebbets Field, in late August
of my eighth year, I watched
him drift under a windblown
pop fly, moving from sunlight
to shadow as he drew near home.

Now, on the first anniversary
of his death, the August night
is wild with mosquitos and bats,
skunk in the compost. A pack of deer
thrashes through tangled hazel
and poison oak as they cross the hill
below its crest in search of water.

Nursing the day's final herbal
concoction against joint pain
and lost sleep, the same drink
I have used all twelve years
of my illness, I tilt my head back
in its battered Dodgers cap to rest
against the slats of an Adirondack chair

as a screech owl's solo whistle
pierces the endless crescendo
of bullfrogs and bumble bees

when Reese at last drifts back out
of evening shadows. He wears
loose flannels. Wrinkled with age,
stained by his long journey,
he still moves with that old grace
over the grass. I see anguish
of long illness on his familiar face
and something like relief too,
that rueful smile, the play finished,

game over. I stand and his arm
settles on my shoulder, a gesture
he used to silence the harrowing
of Jackie Robinson. He helps me
find balance while the world spins
as it always does when I rise
and the whisper of wind is his voice
saying it will be all right, pain is nothing,
stability is overrated, drugs play havoc
with your game, lost sleep only means
waking dreams, and illness is but a high
pop fly that pulls us into shadow.

He is gone as the wind he spoke with
dies down. I find myself on the trail
those deer walked, seeing where I am
now though already lost in a darkness
that soon will reach home.

WINTER SOLSTICE

I wake in darkness and fog to the hoofbeat of deer
racing across the hill's frosted crest from east to west.
As in a dream, within the rise and fall of wind I hear
the rise and fall of the deer pack's breath
as it becomes the beat of my heart within my chest.
I am fitted so close to my wife's body her breath
seems to be my breath as we curl together, awake
but not awake, her back rising against my rising chest
in the lingering pre-dawn dark.
Now, in the space between our breath, silence comes to rest.